TWO HEARTS BEAT

THE POETRY OF

Andy Clausen & Pamela Twining

BACK TO EARTH

Pamela Twining

ACE IN THE HOLE

Andy Clausen

Published by
New Generation Beat Publications

Copyright 2024
by
New Generation Beat Publications

All Rights Reserved

ISBN:978-1-957654-09-6

Raymond Foye - Editing

Danny Shot - Editing

Michael L. Kilday - Editing

Debbie Tosun Kilday - Editing & Cover Design

Human Error Publishing - Editing & Formatting

Cover photo by Marcia Ward

All poems submitted by the authors in this book are owned and copyrighted by each individual author and remains theirs. NBPF thanks each author for including their work here.

New Generation Beat Publications asks that no part of this publication be reproduced or transmitted in any form, or by any means electronic or mechanical, Including photocopy, recording or information storage or retrieval system without permission in writing from New Generation Beat Publications. The reasons for this are to help support the publisher and the artists.

Back To Earth
Pamela Twining

Table of Contents

Back To Earth	7
Duck n Cover	9
you, who were kissed	10
Never That Girl	11
The Best Days	14
A Singular Light	16
Let's Dance	18
Earth Abides	21
California is Burning	22
Northern Lights	23
Thunderbird Boogie	25
Confiteor (I Confess)	29
Jewel's Nest	31
Orgasm	33
Woman of the Lineage	36
Transition	38
Stolen	39
There Is No America	43
Fragment	46
California is Burning (Redux)	47
Rue	50
Skeletons	51
It Was All New	53
Pamela Twining Biography	54

Ace In The Hole
Andy Clausen

Table of Contents

She Dances In Love	57
The Moon In Your Eyes	58
Notes From The Ground Under	59
Independence Day	62
Veracity	65
Joysey	67
Why I'm Limping	70
I Recall Reading It Can Be Done	79
WTF	80
In The Land Of Liberty	83
Bad Bald Eagle	84
Ace In The Hole	87
Andy Clausen Biography	102

Back to Earth

Pamela Twining

Back To Earth

Come back to earth my father said
your feet are sky too high
some things are and some things aren't
no one knows which they are but it's so
it's so
a Lady doesn't stand on her head
ever

we entered the workforce en masse
small jobs necessitated by
moving mechanical parts
by endless paper forms and documents
       documents
semi-literate smart enough to read
not permitted the courtesy
       of being meant to understand it
human copy machines
we wore pants
we fixed things and kept them fixed
while men went to War
our sons fathers and brothers fed to the guns
of Wars for possession of an earth now roiling
in storms droughts migrations and famines
in the age of the spillage of the cornucopia
for Some

they prod us
they pit us against each other in life
and in fantasy control our desires
our deepest held beliefs
keep mindful of Possession
       not Coexistence
             not Preservation
                   not Maintaining
Buying Selling and Fencing Exclusion
Fighting or making the underlings fight
for boundaries drawn by Other wars
       from ancient days

who argues now
about the ascendance of patriarchy
who doubts that superiority
      was achieved and demonstrated
          through acts of war?
and in that commission acts sometimes
of a barbarousness and brutality
it Pales that such ferocity is enamored
by "the mob"
      who are they?
people tired sick to death
desperate often starving
and losing their homes
and their families aborted for Real
in the womb of society
the womb of us Living together on a finite planet

we once marveled at Open Spaces
those windows are closing
except for the estates of the owners
who shield themselves from the crowds
of those Others
the not rich
      not famous
who live at the pleasure of those
who can ask them to give up their lives
for a myth
for a substance black-out of the earth
of the eternal womb
      the only one we know
of a mother who is getting ready
      to Throw Us Out of the House!

Duck n Cover

crouching under desks
      lined up in the halls
how innocent it all seems now
images of Syria ripe in our eyes
we in America have not been
the Children of War in that way
where the desks are blasted to splinters
and the walls to smithereens
the body parts on the playground
      that might have been your friend
a shadow silhouette on the wall
all the imprint of that life
photonegative
ghosts everywhere

you, who were kissed

you, who were kissed
by the maid, Joan of Arc
on the eve of her triumph
so long ago
held aloft by your mother
in the air wild
with bells
offered in joy
to her shining lips
were you branded forever
with the fire of holiness?
did your starved limbs fill out
with the promise of bliss?

touched by the soldier-maid
sent straight from heaven
surrounded by angels
and god, the Electric
did your heart swell triumphant?
Was your voice raised in song?

you, who were brushed
by the passage of destiny
kissed by wonder and joy
one bright night in your youth
held
for a moment
by the hope of a nation
did your soul grow inside you?
did it matter at all?

Never That Girl

I was never That girl
the one w Legs Up To Here
sleek and shining curls exploding
firm flesh sculpted Just Right
lookin Great in any clothes
        that fell out of the sky and landed
                all helter skelter but Perfectly
on her body
That girl all eyes follow
Perfect
Glowing
it's she All the designs are designed For
stiletto heels sheer stockings and fragile silks
skirt hiding little
    (I Did have a dynomite skirt I made from a
    pair of jeans released the inseams and
    sewed a satin panel in the back
    left the front Open Up To ... well
    ... my mother was Not amused but I wore it
    she disowned me
    not really but it was a close thing...
    I wore blue leather platform Boots w studs
    I wore layers of nail polish metallic green
    blue blood red black wore sequins on my
    face and glitter in my hair
        Devine Decadence! as Liza said)

but I was Never That girl
the one All eyes follow as she glides
almost Above the surface of the earth
to wherever she's going and people
        especially men
            walk into walls
        and fall off of curbs
(I was With That girl once and walking
a bit behind her I Watched it happen
Laughed so hard I could Barely walk my own self
it was like an old-time slapstick movie
as if Mae West was gyrating down the street

and the men on the sidewalk
Literally fell off the curb
and/or walked into telephone poles
they couldn't take their Eyes Off of her)

young women in their late teens early 20s
Every One of them Gorgeous
sleek lovely tanned
a few blonde one Latinx an AfAmerican
and my daughter of N8v American heritage
all talking about How Ugly They Were!!
Any One of them could have been in movies
Every one of them had Star Quality!
and me
      plain ol me thinking
how we Do our girls and young women
make them hypercritical of themselves
of their appearance
so that even the Most Beautiful Hate themselves
and see in their mirrors hags & monsters
or Sad Orphans
or too fat too thin too white
too flat too busty
too tall too short too dark too light
too kinky too straight
too big too freckled too plain
too crooked too muscular too hairy
      too too too too!

No Woman I have known
has Ever been Happy with her appearance
even women who Seem to Think they're Beautiful
      are Lying
deep down inside they're Afraid
afraid they're too too too too (see above)
even when they Act like they Think they're All That
way deep down they're cringing
and praying no one notices
how they've been Fooled by the makeup
the dyed hair
expensive well-planned outfits

the jewelry

we must Sparkle men into Oblivion
so they Won't notice the Real Aschenputtel
in the hearth behind the door

The Best Days

days when I don't have to work and
short winter days
where I wear so many layers that no one can tell
and I don't have to wear a bra
always de rigeur to correctly fill out clothing
        to not Bounce

I mean they've always been big
ever since they were anything at all
other than generic nipples
the same as any kid
a little brown not pink from my heritage
suddenly swollen and aching
and dad who used to let me run around without a shirt
      when I was 6
           now hollering at me to pull my top Down

they've always been big
so that my mother was amazed
to realize I wasn't a flat little girl anymore
        8th grade I think
I remember school shopping for jr high
that First time
I wanted a bra
she said I had to wait
till I had something to put in it
which came about with a vengeance
        within a year
and no male ever looked at my face again
eyes glued to my midsection
bust (Never say breasts)
properly covered
yet still obviously way more fascinating
than mere eyes

luckily
it being the 60s and all
I was empowered by the Sexual Revolution
to say and do all things erotic
myself as a woman
        young woman
                adolescente girl
but always very forward
precocious
and as any good scientist
        (which my father wanted me to be)
loved experimentation

by now dad was gone on to another life and
family
still ours but separate
and fraught
with all sorts of undercurrents
of hatred lost love and resentments
second half of childhood paying
their prejudices back
with my bursting rebellion
but also pure love of the games
between men and women
or girls as it was then
        never liked boys my age
                so boring and unadventurous
        still running in packs
not quite ready to slip into a quiet place and
marvel over all the aspects of bodies and their
electricities
        their steaming electricities

A Singular Light

the poetry was Electric
      brought the House Down
dual jagged pillars of Light
Crashing from heaven downward
emblazing the night sky
      smell of ozone pricks nostrils
        eyes opened in
           Shock

Intimate but inherently Of the World
      the Whole world not just our small corner
Revolution/Revelation
poems grow evolve entwine themselves
      (selves yes poems have selves)
in hearts and minds
eyes
settling hidden among the fallen leaves
leavings

of yesterday's apparitions
too busy too driven too preoccupied too resistant
too rebellious rejected remiss
mental leaves rotting detritus
kicked over the pathways
obscuring the gems rough gems
unpolished
you have to un-earth the sparkle

blazing Bolts from heavenly source
God's hand god's hand goddess' hand
the hand of the Creator Mother of All
the Electric
      food of Poets
chipping gently hacking greedily
the Song the Song
the Singer hears each, own
drops gleaming sparks charged
powered
making captives of hungry seekers

hiding
in the caves and sunken grottoes
wildernesses unexplored

tied to the turning wheel
ageless as stones
the Lightning danced among the buildings
    gone beyond gone
in love with the outermost star

Let's Dance

Let's Dance to the End of Everything
the final cries of a Social Generation
as we begin an age of isolation
our skins still soft and Begging
to be touched
our lips our lips
our fleshy selves pulsing
to the desire for Contact
our fleshy selves
the softer parts
not Studying War the gentle parts
demanding Peace
tender but resolute

Let's Dance
imagining the soft collision of Bodies
a Crush of other selves
awash in music
twisting and spinning in the Waves
      the Waves
           Leaps of Faith
Injustice Rules, wherefore then Faith?
it Is in Human Nature to Hope
(... springs eternal for a Reason
      yes it does!)
there are Always those
who Believe in a Just and Conscious Future
a Time of Love Among Being Kind
that was after all
the message of Jesus the Christ

and So we still keep
writing dancing painting making music
still keep doing Art even in Desolation
the Cold and Dreadful Frozen Starved
or the Broiling Skin-Popping Crispy Critters
the End Result of unfiltered sunlight on the surface
Dig Deep
      Dig Deep

is that the only way to Come Together
in the Mines?
tunnel down down
down through mycelium mast and mould
through foetid dank and loamy Earth
Soaked with punishing rains
(not punishment for the living beings anchored in the soil
they Belong)
it's We who are the Secret
the Unnamed
the Uninvited
the Storm Troopers taking Over all the habitat
and killing land and sky
destroying Water
poisoning the Wells of Kindness Strength and Mercy
in pursuit of Mammon

can we Live without Sunlight under ground
away from a Sun now Deadly
sneak up-surface twice a month
for Ceremony Moon Tide
mångata the mystic path
North to Moon
through ether to the Mother
to disappear in Welcoming Arms

And it Really Was a Game
Congratulations All Around and Thanks
just those of US who Thought it was Life left hanging
w our jaws scraping the tarmac
No Way as even ones we Trusted Most
began to High Five and Celebrate
the ascendance of one who's Less
So Much Less than what was Dreamed
and those Pragmatic sunzabitches
Insist there's nowhere else to go
        I Beg to Differ

Let's Dance!
for Children whose memories
      are Locked Away
for elders waiting withering wanting
Touch Denied
Let's Dance!
for a planet pulsing to new life
in spite of All
for the End of the Road in Sight
for all the Love we forgot to give
for all the Laughter at the cosmic joke
Let's Dance!

Earth Abides

the Time of No Time
Mother Shaking to her Core
a Time of Madness and of Spirit

the monsters that walk amongst us
the fires of their hatreds burn Unceasing
but the seed the fruit will live longer

germinate in Utter Silence
Darkness mulch and mould mycelia Life
even in the oppressive heat
of a plague summer

treating others' bodies as if they
were their Own
touch designed as if to Claim a Right
out into the Night mists rising darkening

in a time when there are no Roads
paths create themselves
in a time when there are no Clocks
        Imagine

I taste the depths of you breathe you in
swirl obscure completing the Darkness
swift blade of the Dark

this is your Dance no water no food
thank God if there is a God or gods
for you

jealous of the Rain caressing your skin
wanting your touch above all things
spill the last of your life into me

what we undertake for each other
This Dance, No hesitation No Fear
I acknowledge the Light in you

and Earth Abides

California is Burning

protecting his wife from a bully
shot while backing away
he went back inside
and died on the floor
in front of his five-year-old child
license to kill in America

Broken Hearts, Broken Minds
the caged children emerge
disconnected the emptiness of eyes
deep pools of lost memories
suffering with no recourse
the magic of loving touch dispersed
in darkness

the sun poured down
impossible liquid buttercup
sunflower warm melted gold
heaven's wealth sliding sinuously
enveloping earthbound
should have been joyous reaching upward
to bathe engulf immerse all
in sweet drawn butter molten
incomprehensible Love held in stillness
but slipping away momentarily
such an ineffably beautiful world
unless there are no windows no doors
cinderblock walls painted to look like outside
a deep horror of false color and light

I heard that half of American youth
Have never heard of Auschwitz
no wonder the light is fading
we all bleed inside each other's wounds
the wells of memory shallow
in spite of centuries
silt washes down from chosen ignorance
to fill obscure delude
remove the mirrored depths
source of reflection

Northern Lights

glorious icy January late afternoon
breath fails me
watching the snowflakes spark
like fireflies in the cold winter sun
fairy rainbows disappearing in a nano

best thing about winter afternoons
they transform into night so sweetly
       goldens fading
            to infinite shadings of grey
slipping down to silver-limned blacknesses
then jagged sharp ice knife surprising
bone-chilled limbs
   cocooned under piles of blankets
      watch final light fade from the sky
      and the dark surrounds
         last edges lit with blue-fire rays
boreal lights shifting colors
      magic and cold thrusts
         stabbings
an icicle to the heart but melts
in the heat of our coming together

the dreams I have
still crackling with electricity
young
spicy
the scent of you
nerve endings spark juices flow
ignite!
and you are laid waste again
     at my mercy again
and I can't help but call you to me

let me touch you
let me feel the stories etched across your life
let me call forth All
your own dreams and memories
     share all with me

      I am so greedy

we can still Dance that bed across the room my love

Thunderbird Boogie

I. The Argument

autumn air crisp and clean
mountains dressed in gold
and russet
evergreen spikes interrupt holiday clad hills
scent of the dying old year
sweet and smoky
warmer than years gone by
the climate altering our round of days

I take off layers of scarves and jackets
fall teasing my nostrils with chill promises
but summer haunts the hillsides
not giving in to expectations
occasional surprise of flowers unblemished by frost
or even the sudden snowstorm that came the other day
sparkle spot of crimson orange violet
violent explosion of life that tells me
everything has changed
is changing
that unseasonable soft warm sudden breeze
shimmer shakes unfallen leaves
music of a world in flux
the veil between hard world cosmos rent and gone

what have we done?

living out the blessings of the past
while stealing futures unknown and unsung
our fortunes blind
we gratefully accept what is not ours to take

so many lives I cannot know so many places I'll never go
the shimmering buzzing ghosts of bees

brought to death by human machination
grows
expands
   fills ears and eyes
drowning cries of those whose lives destroyed
by hunger war the need for flight
and in that endless running
homes societies torn down apart

Ratatatat!!
the guns
mangled bodies
the dead cities
starving wasted limbs and giant liquid eyes

who has looked into the eyes of the children of war?

not I, in my golden cocoon
as nests of poisonous snakes multiply unseen beneath my feet
fed by greed and willful ignorance
no predators left
the forests have fallen to the giant teeth
the grasping jaws
of those given license by some made up god
whose fabled grant of Dominion usurps natural law

the knowledge of the Old Ones tossed aside
like worn out shoes
ancient wisdom torn and spat upon

Money knows Best!

II. The Vision

I saw a charnel land
isles of death
the blackened stalks and stumps
the silent skies
world waiting for the end of days for human-
kind
the heart of the cannibal giant
dreamed into being by the worst natures
dark lords of hate and envy

from Lovelock Cave the Si-te-cah poured forth
and Danced
in the forests raging ragged redhead pale faces
swelling with greed
heart-fed veins black snakes beneath the soil
blood black viscous
defiling the land the crops and water
hundreds of unknown and unmarked spills of
blood and oil
the tops of mountains gobbled by the great
maw of the eater of worlds
the State's private army pollutes the ceremo-
nies
ravages the prayers
persecutes the most powerful of the powerless
anyone whose humbling
will make the State appear potent

earth's children running naked from the flame
breath
dragon breath
earth's children standing
like stones
block passage of the snake's foul head

the cold dead world
no food for the living
yet incubates seeds of life deep within
shrugging away the takers

flicking off like fleas
like lice
crushed beneath boulders heaved by the Mother's
giant roar

Enough!

she calls on Thunderbird
Great southern condor
to cast his vast shadow over the land
to circle and spiral and dive
snatch up the hydra!

the snake coiling pregnant with black death
spilling deathblood deep into soil and water

Enough!

will we be as the numberless stars Rising
immutable
or will his wings blot out the sky?
The Dance of the Thunderbird has begun

Confiteor (I Confess)

it was my fault
for being young female and alone
on dark streets
it was my fault
for speaking to a man I didn't know
it was my fault
for wearing shorts tight jeans fitted slacks
a gauzy skirt a long skirt a short skirt
it was my fault
for thinking it was just a friendly conversation
it was my fault
for letting him buy me a drink
it was my fault
for walking home from the bus stop at night
it was my fault
for not being violent enough
for not screaming loud enough
for being so scared no sound would come out at all
it was my fault, it was my fault, it was my fault

I confess I bare my soul I bury my soul
I tell the almighty powers
the police the teachers my parents
and they tell me it was my fault
that I shouldn't have been there
that I shouldn't have worn that
that I should have been home
that I should have been studying
that I should have been decently silent
that I never should have laughed
accepted that drink
walked down that street
you get what you ask for
you get what you deserve

I have sinned exceedingly
in thought word and deed
and my judges are men and mock-virgins

women who have never looked outside the world
described by patriarchy
defined by the judges
men whose hands are not clean
women who have never questioned the boundaries
because when they stepped outside, they were punished
much the same as I will be
the only forgiveness is Silence
the only forgetting is Silence
the Silence is Deafening

mea culpa, mea culpa, mea maxima culpa

Jewel's Nest

in all the Deep of Night
when even stars have gone to bed
Black like the lining of a jewel box after the jewel is gone
Dead Black
no supporting contrast gleam
of diamond
emerald
topaz
ruby
Fathomless Black
the sad outcome of drownings
smotherings
loss of all that was known in Life
that passage that no one has breached on the way back
to let us know what lies Beyond the Dark

so many times I lie and watch you sleep
your chest rising
yes! and yes!
each inhalation a miracle that keeps us joined
for long and long
I hear your muttered dreamings
touch and taste your skin like angel wings
so softly you never know
give thanks each night for the miracle
that came to us both in later times
when cynicism Might have been expected
to dull our knowledge and acceptance of True Love
years unknown to each other
breeze in ghostly tatters
behind a constant testimony
that there were other lives before We Were
some aspects gone and missed
some gone, not missed at all

it's Dark

in all the Deep Deep Black of Night
the Dark Hole that swallows Universes beckons
as I pull away and confront the mirror
only to see my Grandmother
Not my Grandmother
but I

so she was
her honey golden skin paled and mottled
russet hair now silvered down and thinner
than once exuberant curls
her youthful ebullience
studied insouciance
weathered to a leathery acceptance
of limits never Dreamed of in her youth
a time when we walked Hard upon the earth
Knowing we were the First people
of consequence
to arrive
that we would ever be remembered
as the Healers of Mankind
not having come yet to the conclusion
that the very Word
Erased
over half of the species so designed

that Now am I
standing at the edge of the Void
still knowing and loving
still thinking and striving
on the border of "going gentle" and Raging
into the Night the Eternal
where each one's footsteps go alone
the other side of the Dark
ever Unknown
save only met in Blazing Love
as I have felt with you
the Circle completed
the jewel Dancing Fire
at the core of the Darkness
like Life unending

Orgasm

the sublime validation of this incarnation
embodiment of this set
of yearnings
and completions
is not necessary for women
in the scheme of procreation
many thirsting as for a distant dream
though they have borne
and nurtured infants at their breasts

clitoridectomy
infibulations
ritual removal of the pleasure center
from the yoni
Sacred Base
the connection with Original Mother
to whom we return Blood
and eventually Flesh and Bone
yet receive no possibility of delight
in that foul excision

they are surely saints
whose lives rise above such denials
"possessing the Secret
Of Joy"
deep within the body memory
in the flesh in the cells
in the Meat of our beginnings
before the Flood buried all the ancient stories
before the desert sands welled up
tsunamis
swallowing the cradles of the gods
the First People
whom rumor is
will also be the Last

in estrus
a girl just scratches that itch
until she's pregnant

no explosive "O My God"!!s
precede the cosmic joining
of horse sperm and ovum
or cheetah or Great Ape
zygotes of cats and dogs
were not conceived in Love
were not sanctioned in Ceremony
were not the result of meeting
someone Hott! in a bar
a candlelit dinner and a movie
the honor of Family
the saving of Face among friends
the wish for a secure future
the conscious fulfillment
of Destiny

femina sapiens is the only female
Known to be orgasmic*
(if not multi-orgasmic)
It can't just be
so she won't walk away
spunk running down her legs
upright as she is
or why
do they only get Better
with age?

what profit orgasm
for those whose seed is wizened
diseased or lacking
for whom childbirth
is only memory or regret?

ejaculate conserved
is stardust of billennia
released
the seed will be broadcast on the water
spilled in the rich mould
of the forest floor
the body cavities
of men and women

no more barren

a supreme act of Choice
hold back
as tantric babas say
and Energy! Enlightenment!
crashing in the waves
of involuted comings
Songs so consummate and silent
even the candles of the midnight sky
shimmer and blaze in Awe

Woman of the Lineage

the mystery of writing before paper
vellum parchment oratory
dying now
letters like tombstones
becoming a thing of the past
there can be no more burials
no more vast fields of grey stones
each with its own tale
mumbling together
the murmur of the bones
unquiet souls trapped
in impermeable boxes under soil
unless they can escape quickly enough
the decaying corpus

Pyres or Sky Burials release the Spirit
all at once
feed the futures in song & story
but there can be no more
fields of the dead
unless we Rent the space
or pile others on top

no more burials
no more stone memorials
symbolic art and loving passages
carven imagery and rhythm
rhyme
Lost to random futures
the ashes blown away on winds
the bones the leaves the pages burned
no Homer
no Shakespeare
no Jesus the Christ
all these icons don't exist
are amalgams of
are composites

a collusion of poets
no single person whose brilliance
brings one to great heights
but a historical gathering
of poets and singers taking years
even decades
to compose

the Poet Commune
shared over time and space
pulling love and regret from the ether
pulling bravery and derring-do from the void
does it make it More cosmically Special
if there is One Poet
All that Wisdom and Verse emanating
from One Heart, One Mind
or is the Brilliance observed in the Collective
the passing of poesis
transmission of image and color across Aeons,
across generations?

is it necessary that that transmission
be in some sense physical
as in the Lineage
of sexual relationships among poets
from Whitman to Peter Doyle to Gavin Arthur
to Neal to Ginsberg to Peter
to Janine to Andy
to Me

Transition
– for RB, 1/20/19

this tranquil January morning
impressions of cold grey sojourns
in the windy silence
redolent of rain
      wet earth
           and mourning lonely
after the crowds have gone

the human spirit surrounds one like vapor
      tasteless
and all that's good consumed by hungry earth
now the flame of mind's dispersed

Fall away Fall away
buried beneath winter's mast
like a leaf from an earlier slaughter
the hollow shell of a nut
food for worms

darkens the day
senses fade
experience denied

when the scent of new mown grasses
      the touch of wind on skin
          the color green
no more delight

Stolen

the secret music of the children tears my flesh
spirit journeys of a newer time unknown
in dreams all empty nights long
darkness
without pity
the lost children
the ones whose poetry is untried
bare limbs torn from mothers
torn from homes and lives
torn from the breasts of those
who only wanted to give them more and better
the abject tortured poems cried in the dark
innocent/not innocent
        Terror

the death of journeys
death of hope
the echoes of the heart
the deepest memories
the never
never
never
our land forgotten
left behind with older dreams
with Nothing but barren fields
empty streets and tumbling cots
wizened shrunken faces
of the ancient ones
sprung from the soil
roots deep in a place called Home

haunted sleepless obscured night skies
stars lost in lowering bleakness
no moon to give us back
the songs we left that place with
and disembodied footfalls
loud voices
words not understood
and then the tearing and the screams

and then the blackness falls all round
the soundless dreams crushed together
with no language
driven
beaten
    broken on the lathe of hell
the horror of those moments
when we believed the good
the open loving arms
arms now tearing
demanding
no whispered loving sounds
but taunts and hideous laughter
as force gives up no names
no identities
no longer innocent
nightmares without names or faces
the screams filling all orifices
leaving no room for light
the holes left in bodies
psyches
spirits
deep wells bottomless
in the night of cries and evil almost-whispers
like grinding gears or ripping clothes
deadly whispers calling ugly names
and putting hands where hands should never be
soft untouched skin
deep gravid eyes
wounded with forgetting
wounded with the need for oblivion

what will become of these children
calling out their agonized refrains
in the deepest time of night
where dreams go to die
the promised borning burning
torched by invective
the delicate skin
the trembling flesh
words ripped from center

by naked claws
ever since the mother was torn away

where is the mother, the father
where?
do they not love me ever any more
why don't they come
where is that lullaby
that song that let me sleep at last
why did they go and leave me here?
with just this crying
endless crying
words are told to me but all is din
discord
voices layered and overlapping
hard hands and harsh impatient touch
names lost
exchanged for numbers

I, in safety
hear
and plead for torture to stop
there is no remedy, no sanctuary
and the poetry of children tears my soul
I am complicit
my age will not forgive me
I am not forgiven
tears fall and mingle
with rivers and lakes of laments
unceasing streams
weeping for what's been taken
there's no giving back
it's gone
fragile lives melt into other lives
and older times
forgotten times
the young hatched from these caged birds
know no sacred touch
no love
can words half remembered
buried deep within the memories of long ago

when mother held them
her soothing bell-like voice
sang sweet unworded nothings
into tiny shell-like ears
the promises
lost promises given
can forgotten words still heal?

we can only give them poetry
and broken promises
but maybe poetry will be enough

There Is No America

there Is No America as we believed it to be
as we have been trained raised taught to know;
US History begins in Freedom
Flight from Persecution
and the establishment of a Free Country

Free to Individuals Bold enough
Determined enough
Blessed enough
to Claim their Rights under a Constitution
ostensibly written to cover "All Men" in the generic
only excluding those Not Defined as Men
NDNs Black people and Women (Of Course!)
and by that Very assumption made the Ideal
Impossible to achieve

another account of the founding of US
the Dark side
that Slave labor was Necessary
that Red Savages Must Be Driven Out
if we can't Cheat em we make em Sick
if they Still Hang on Invade em
Push em to Violence defending their lands
their grounds their territories
the source of their Food
their Traditional Ceremonies

their Homes must give way to US
Must give way
Murders Were Committed

our Black Sisters and Brothers
after their Liberation from the bonds
of Generations of servitude
forced lives Stolen
a brief heady Time of Real Freedom
looking around to the Possibilities of Everything
then Jim Crow flew in and the Twisted Triple Ks

and Freedom only meant Free to Suffer and Die
dangling from a tree battered and tortured
at the hands of Hatred
hands of Judgement
hands of Anger at the Servant
Elevated to the Realm of their "Betters"
and then what do They have?
what do they have but the same Grim Prospects
as their erstwhile slaves
enslaved people Not Even Owned by most
who were too poor to actually Own a slave
but Aspiring to do so one day
a proper Goal for a Rich White man
and Now those former servants
Some White Someone's former servants
Might be richer than you
more respected than you
such a thing is Unconscionable

Fly Away Jim Crow!
Free Leonard Peltier!
Remember that Water is Sacred!
Water is Life!
Remember the Homeland was Homeland to
Others
before you unjustly drove out
penned in
hunted down
pushed Beyond the newly Created Boundaries
of this Nation/that Nation
Never before acknowledged in the world of
hunter gatherers
you Go where the Food is
follow the hoofprints pawprints
find the bee tree
chase fish upstream
territory only defined by relations
with local tribes

now there are invisible Lines
drawn through the land

trees and stones mark where you can
no longer go
they signed treaties that were filled with lies
expressions of good faith
that turned out to be Laughable
if you could stop Crying long enough
they signed Hopeless treaties because what else
could they do?
That or be expunged from the Face of the Earth
sent Nameless to the Great Beyond
Without Honor
the sad thing is that the Deep State is Real
there Is No America as we believe it to be

.

Fragment

life always returns
in one form or another
unless or until it doesn't
my prayers are for future generations
our children to the 7th generation
who will see the devolution
of societies
of polities
economies
and experience the anomie
that has always been at the edge of the broken
world
inhabited by poets and dreamers

tangled roads of history winding
through the unplumbed depths of Now
temples to godhead built
from the stones and bones of the Mother
the voices of eons of souls
interred in her capacious womb
crying out for remembrance
as memory crumbles away
birdsong like glass shards sparking the electric
dawn
leviathan asphalt skin suffocates the clamor
the demands to acknowledge the fine roots
the web of tomorrow's juicy appetites

darkness falls like an act of mercy
how far can you fall into Nothing or roll away
the stone from the cave of the heart
loneliness of a shooting star burns a trail
the maddening smile of the Void

I touch the hieroglyphics of your skin with my
fingertips
hills and hollows
ridges scars and rough spots
like a blind woman learning Braille
seeking answers to whispered questions

California is Burning (Redux)

California is Burning
Brazil is On Fire
Australia in Flames
one can't be a poet and be silent
broken words shatter worlds
with lies
stories told retold
compelling fantasies of life
as it was wished to be
seen through veils of childhood dreams
meanwhile too many
have had their eyes closed
forever

shielding his wife from a bully
    shot while backing away
he went back inside
    and died on the floor
        in front of his five-year-old child
Stand Your Ground!
license to kill in America

Broken Hearts, Broken Minds
the caged children emerge
    disconnected
the emptiness of eyes
    deep pools of lost memories
        suffering with no recourse
the magic of loving touch dispersed
in darkness

the sun poured down
impossible liquid buttercup
sunflower warm melted gold
heaven's wealth sliding sinuously
enveloping the earthbound
should-have-been-joyous reaching upward
to bathe engulf immerse all
in sweet drawn butter molten

    incomprehensible Love held in stillness
        but slipping away momentarily
            such an ineffably beautiful world
unless there are no windows no doors
cinderblock walls painted to look like outside
        a deep horror of false color and light

Indonesia is in Flood
Puerto Rico is Drowning
Millennial Rains fall without end
Africa's soil is cracked and dry
even the rich are carrying buckets from the well
the melting arctic permafrost releasing
long dormant diseases of ancient days
vast movements of people shifting
from ancestral lands
the cries of family bones ignored
that the family may survive

I heard that half of American youth
have never heard of Auschwitz
        no wonder the light is fading
we all bleed inside each other's wounds
the wells of memory shallow
in spite of centuries
silt washes down from chosen ignorance
to fill
obscure
delude
remove the mirrored depths
all source of reflection

California is Burning
Brazil is On Fire
Australia in Flames
Indonesia's in Flood and Puerto Rico Trembling
Shuddering as Earth tries to shake us off
billions of creatures
whole species Lost
our Final century dawns
unknown, unacknowledged

if Death has a memory
she will Sing for us at the End
Yonnondio!

Rue

Woman of Sorrows
Ophelia
drowned hair floating among the weeds
slashing with her jagged edges
the drums talked in her bones
but she couldn't interpret
what they said

she'd loved the world once
so Alive
everything Wild
gripped tightly between thighs
but that last time
the last time
they made love heavy & slow
like people under water
breathless

tied to the turning wheel
she knew
that no one is remembered
that they always carry their own tombstones
inside them

Do you feel the vastness though?
And just how fleeting every moment is?

the moon a thread of light against the sky
lightning dancing on the horizon
gone beyond gone
she could still move mountains

the moments of a life preserved in stone
grass grown mound
faded inscription
the cost of freedom
buried
in the ground

Skeletons

secrets
old and buried
stories never told to anyone
too deeply underground
desiccated
covered with a carpet of lies
covered with a blanket of self-delusion
the youth we were
the myths and legends
we convinced ourselves of
it Was the way it was
no questions
how complicated life is once the web is wound
and we are caught in sticky tendrils
of our own extrusion
struggling for a moment
then giving in to the inevitable

it becomes easy to erase the realities of the past
and blanket them with sweet nothings
they become like ancient puzzles
pieces worn
edges chipped and rounded
lost memories packed away
in the attic of childhood
the picture no longer whole
shapes purposely whittled away to fit
the narrative we chose

and what of Truth?
what of the bright and shining verities?
the open innocent candor?

ghosts materialize before our eyes
their shades displaying forgotten honor
the death of love and trust overshadowing
sparkling lie
distracting all with a believable fiction
and that's what we lived with all these years

only now recognizing what we've done
the righteous reality revealed
in all its unremembered splendor

we were innocent once
but took that to the grave
of our youth and indecision
we made up our minds
to remember the alterations
not the original garment
like making a disguise
out of costume
out of whole cloth

like a naked emperor
whose story is finally done

It Was All New

it was all new
skin soft and fuzzed
like a bursting peach
ready to spill juice at lightest touch
muscles taut beneath Hard from working
become more grizzled
as we grow older in our days and years

but tactile memory
like photograph found and unaware
the springy curls of your belly again beneath my hand
and touching tasting the root of your desire
small gasps and moans
sweet torture nipping at your secret places

a miracle every day to look at you and remind myself
that you love me

Pamela Twining

traveled the US with her partner, poet Andy Clausen, performing her work in California, Colorado, New York City, Michigan, Wisconsin and places in between. Her work had appeared in Big Scream, Big Hammer, PoetryBay, The Café Review, Napalm Health Spa, and Heyday!, among others. With Andy Clausen, she is co-curator of The Invisible Empires of Beatitude page at The Museum of American Poetics (www.poetspath.com) and for several years, she co-produced the Janine Pommy Vega Poetry Festival in Woodstock, NY, where she and Clausen resided. She was the author of four chapbooks, i have been a river...(2011), utopians & madmen (2012), A Thousand Years of Wanting; the Erotic Poetry of Pamela Twining (2013) and Renegade Boots (2019). In 2021, she and Andy Clausen released a "flip book", a joint publication of Never That Girl (Pamela) & From Oakland to Eternity (Andy).

Pamela Twining
State of New York Beat Poet Laureate
(2022-2024)
November 27, 1950 - July 8, 2023
RIP

Ace In The Hole
Andy Clausen

She Dances In Love
(after Byron)

"She walks in beauty"
She signals the Future
She'll be a formidable friend
She is a magic lover
She glides in grace
with flocking birds
in the tickling sunlight
She spins solar system topography
She waltzes with companies of snowflakes
chorusing the sound track
the visual memory
the smells & noise of new puberty
She climbed into a branch to see
what she had been missing
Her monthly blood reminded
her what was unpursued
She boogies with an entire nation
Her arms stiffen
Her eyes flame
Her cheeks sparkle
Her smile grins symphonic light
Her cradle is warm & total
She walks in Beauty
& Dances in Love

The Moon In Your Eyes

Let everyone's ideas for peace and prosperity
overwhelm my verse
I must conceive only schemes & plans
that can work
not all can, we know that
Fluidity of body conviction
Where the Beulah Land Leaper has naturally
perfectly aimed foot into an ocean of fog
The heavy winded cries & moans
of night time forays
Moving in the money never sleeps
In lonesome A M ears to regard
My handle the light & gravity of flesh
like a deranged symphony – infinite insects
incessant buzzings contain the developed
legends of human origins

Gold is the hue of most soothe
Blue is gold's proxy
Your hand wants to touch me in sleep
"I who have nothing adore you"
Want to hold you sleep with you
Sleep inside you
Silver in the clouded horizon
Gold in the middle of the Warm
Mother sky
Constellation sparkling drops more precious than
diamonds
More powerful than the doctored deed
to the resources of earth – your eyes
in a mirror
The moon in your eyes
we are dancing through
our lives once again

Notes From The Ground Under
– recent assessments

To state the ordinary in an extraordinary manner
To describe the extraordinary with ordinary lexi-
con
Rumble Rumble the house is humble
I feel like the Muse is demanding I write
about failure as if it were success
What feels like a stove burn
is a sore from inside
Caused by skeletal man tandeming
the exterior guy's fingers & feet
elbows & neck trying to satisfy
new directions
Using my body as raiment
The fingertips sting like fileted meat
like giant paper cuts

There were brave men living before Agamemnon
There were beautiful women of words before
Sappho
There have always been old ideas showing up
novel
Always visual exuding splattering color variations
Demanding nomenclature & meter to suit the
beat
Of the feet maintaining the lines of succession for
Why?
what the mind hides is exposed in the act
Of cloaking or other deceptions

The goals of democracy
The greed the never sated greed
The greed of the GOP will kill
The goals of Democracy
The DNC seems incapable of not assisting the
GOP!

The goals of Democracy dance across
blue arêtes and warm themselves

on the necessary golden flames
emanating red white glowing embers
The goals of Democracy hate to hear hunger
> of penury children of orphaned devalued
> by lucre by numbers by self perpetuating
neglect and superstitious religion
That hunger's pleas desperate prayer pain
Covering cloud silence in backrooms
with leaden desolate guilt

The Aim of Democracy
Think true generous justice in every facet of life
The Goals of Democracy pick leaders who put the goals
of all (though sadly sometimes only the majority)
(the successful & the underdogs) above
their own interests
The goals of Democracy are golden not bronze
not iron nope & it's the color not the mineral?
The goal of Democracy is a voice & say in both
collective & individual destiny
A responsibility for our species
for our millenniums of culture
The unpopular yet harmless is allowed space &
its sister time, but unpopular is costly
& meagerly appreciated
Who knows the Future?

That thanksgiving won't be a mockish self-deception
as families argue the spoils
& pelf of the land of Natives of the labor
of slaves & vagrancy conscription
wage indenture big time
This does not quite fulfill the Holiday Spirit
They profess gratitude, for the Calvary?
to the rescue of settlers & pioneers
Andy Jackson's Exterminating SS?
Custer, Kit Carson, Manifested Destiny?

Democracy is more than Freedom to quit a job

It's the freedom to inaugurate enterprise born
with the right to air, food shelter opportunity
Democracy never infallible & not always morally
beneficial a scan or delve of history recorded
abuse is clear
Yes tech made it
possible for us to multiply like not since
a long time: prehistory
Tech made it possible to multiply so
but it also has created joblessness
The economy says we're not needed
in such numbers
yet the DNA(one might modify with "good old"
DNA)
maintains a driven foot to the metal blasting
arias
of "me, me, ME! Reproduces MY descendants
helm
& oar the ship of Civilization
Who lives who gestates delivers sires & births
reproduces
decides by whom or what is best
for the productive unselfish majority
in the continuation
of human civilization
Threatens to be decided by war
or other catastrophe
How do we get to a more manageable amount
or how can we up production of life essentials
without polluting and destroying more environs?

Independence Day

I invoke Moitrin & Nitzozos
to aid me to stomach quasi-legal
erratic fireworks growling grievances
Like bombs sounded then showers of neon
flowers & shards of luminescent
gems ooohed and aaahed twinkling
into burnt gun powder void endless
darkness the ashen odor Gone
the explosion still enskulled vibrato over toning
The exuberance of power obtained by expansive
slaughter & subjugation of the ordinary
peasant forced to battle
the manufactured thunder
I shudder like a frightened child even
a whining scared dog at the arterial
ancestral popping pows
(Though I do my damndest to not let show)
Is it artillery?
dropped from a plane?
a drone?
Frigid brews and dogs dressed in spiced mustard
& blood tomato puree & sugar vinegar
I'm having an orange sunshine flashback
just what is this stuff?
Is it food?
Crack the bat on the melon ball
The call for the relay peg to a sliding second
High-pitched screams like the dismissal
of pre-pubic school
Recess jubilation midst the splashing man made
nature altered lakes canals still clear tarns
The unfurled pennants honoring millions
of early savage deaths & wounds of limbs
& scars of heart & tribal vision
The infrequent cousins related to, sharing macaroni
The Wagneresque artilleries & roar of Harleys
& Asian built gas combusting steeds & pickups
of both prosperity & penury
claiming the myriads of highways

The rivers of rural routes rumbling with ready
rude cacophonous swamping concertos
creaming the growing amazing maize
California's veggies raw steamed grilled fried
every state & corner Alaska to Florida
Austin to Honolulu, O yeah artichokes!
Golden State realize & activate your common
sense benevolent spiritual-economic Corso
advocated untamed unbroken unbrokered
POWER!
An old soot faced wrinkly Bo bowing and bending
tunes of ancient Sumer & heroic Greece
on his well-oiled one-man carpenter saw
The drummer has arrived I hear sharp the snare
rim shots revel the bevel shake the devil
Paunchy aging guitar pickers wrench out
Hendrix emulating mangled string scream notes
Senior sex laden saxophones from Elkhart Indi-
ana
encouraging bumping hips undulating pelvis
vibrating breasts oscillating ancestral drums
and astral traveling keyboards
Bud Powell & Little Richard
The Fats: Waller & Domino
Slim Galliard, & Nina Simone
Nina your self knowing talented dignity
& righteous anger I revere
And your physical Beauty!
O Slim you crack me up
O do You! Gleeful Admiration!
Saves a bit of what was prophesied
for me in Leaves of Grass &
At The Top Of My Voice!
Transcending just for a bright moment
Viva the Viva! Bright moments Bright moments!
VIVA THE VIVA BRIGHT IT IS
Despite political omens
of Doom & Damnation
IT'S THE 4TH OF JULY
FREE FREE FREEDOM!
STINGING SINGING RINGING

BRINGING SWINGING ZINGING
SLINGING EMNANCIPATION VIVA!
UNITED MANUMISSION PROCLAIMING
EXCLAIMING VIVA THE VIVA
IT'S THE 4TH OF JULY

Veracity

Truth no longer matters
it is the perception of it
paramount to quenching
the struggle thirst for significance
Significance defined as the Power
to Dominate
Alas for survival the Truth is
often false
Especially in the fabled upside down
shape shifting chaos preceding
the crunching insufferable weight
of the Iron Heel
Truth is the word up for grabs
Truth like a bucking bull with Mike Tyson
deltoids named Do-As-You're-Told fluctuating
oscillating buck jerking busting out of hiding
eyes smoking glaring connotation
in adamant opposition to its denotation
Its Roots, its journey, its evolvements
what it absorbed in times under
imperial bondage & torture
In the desecrating emasculating ungenerous
centuries festering wounds to all
Truth was the first necessity of agreement
It seemed nothing of objectivity would
be used/possessed if it did not exist
It seemed a word whose meaning
could not change
Truth be told it did over & over again
Over time this observation exonerated
the minds of the manipulators
who think they own & command it.
In Truth the Truth changes
like the stock market
The eye, logic, photographs, written
testimony, machine readings, scientific
assiduousness illumination of possibilities
your own eyes none of it is
a major influence on the flow

chart of Truth
One may affect the style of Truth's
public appearance but other factors
beyond control of the masses
are inured and omnipotent over
both sword and fountain pen

Truth I've said you a liar
perhaps too harsh?
But your vague-try
and lethal sadism
Make it difficult to believe in you
therefore believe in anything
A being realizes her aging finiteness
wonders if she had believed lies
All those times around the sun
All that devotion & reliance
Where was the Truth of it?
So Truth I address You
It sure seems like You have
been quite a liar
It's been said You hurt
You hurt me
It was a much easier rise
with a heart juicing flooding
limbs & extremities
When I thought you were
honest & Trustworthy
righteous & Real

Joysey

It didn't take long for me to see
you were the Lou Gehrig of States
A persevering dependable powerhouse
in the shadow of Ruthian NYC
From the farmers & commuters
of the fertile Delaware gap to the
birthplace of baseball, Hoboken
ancient launching pad of the legendary
Hobos who took to the west bound rails
when the economy would sour
Hoboken with that every day, how-can-one
take-it-for-granted, glorious view of Manhattan

The Pocono mountains, fecund valleys, it's famous
Atlantic shore, and buildings from every
prosperous wave of 200 years, impressive
Yet it is your everyday people that taught
a California
boy like me, to love you
From all continents, every culture, religion,
and complexion they came for work
maybe a backyard & little garden
This is where the "Old World" neighborhoods
start melting into "America"

When I first came to you, Hoboken was relatively
inexpensive, 1980
I saw an apartment house on fire
Read the headlines, the council meetings
packed with forced gentrification protest
I gasped when I first saw the sci-fi refineries
from the Turnpike the ominous sordid flames
and miasmic spume--
I surmised that all of Jersey
was similar at the time little did I
know that a legendary poet Hersch Silverman
ran a neighborhood candy store in Elizabeth
and there was plenty of magnificent "Nature"

a short drive into the geography
From the stately wind worn mansions
along the Shore to the crowded hub bub
of Jersey & Union City, the urban toughness
of Trenton & Camden
Home to hundreds of poets, WC Williams, Ginsberg, many Barakas,
Whitman, E. Katz, Patti Smith, Springsteen, Danny Shot, Roskos,
Wiler & Weil, Janine P Vega
yes Joyce Kilmer & many more
and their myriad offspring to come
In 1980 at Long Branch my kids found
thousands of white shells, but not shells
plastic sanitary applicators
When I followed Danny's turnpike towed vehicle
to Perth Amboy, on the bus, arriving
I thought I'd arrived at the "Twilight Zone"
like a movie of city life at least 25 years ago
A nowhere as glamorous as "Grease"
Back in Hoboken a Pizza proprietor picks me
out from his customers to tell what his years
in federal lock-up were like
showed me his scrapbook
At the Northern border with the "Empire State"
I met the 44-year-old chief of the eclectic Ramapough tribe
"In my tribe I am an elder"
From their mountain we could see the big modern
hotel where once the vast Ford factory produced
thousands of jobs & the pollution that's sickening &
killing the mixed race Ramapough to this day
What tales from decades past will I hear
in the Pine Barrens? The dandelion fields
of Vineland?
I never minded the strong coffee roasting odors
wafting from north Hoboken factories
now condos and offices
Every time I drive by the Bendix diner I get
a warm feeling, in fact all the diners
and their pickles, the folk a lot like myself

in the manifold diners & taverns
like Maxwells, The Beaten Path, Court Tavern
"Hungarian" bars of NB, The Malibu
Greasy Tony's, The Melody, a poetic
& rock n roll history juggernauting the Double
Cross century, believe it or not_

I can be seduced by the same marinara
Sinatra loved
I can walk the same ground as Aaron Burr
The Patterson Falls where Allen Ginsberg's
verse declaimed within the sound of water
rumbling crashing roughly singing
"Capitol Air" Yes the waterfall
singing Ginsberg!

I think of the Hindenburg in flames
Rubin Carter, Jack Wiler, Long Shot magazine
I think of the 98.6% who got their start here
Weehawken, HoHoKus, Secaucus, Mahwah
Jersey & Union City, Tom's River, Exit 13, Wayne
I see their faces and hear their voices
to this day in this night

Why I'm Limping

The Brightness ordered me to stop working
"Safety First" over in the maple shade
The Union Hall of the clouds instructed me
to milk the jetsam and flotsam comprising
my pummeled mind
to play the organ to hear it
in a dim night club
round about midnight
in my head behind my eyes
in the shreds of my mind in my mind
behind my eyes
Where I was baptized against my will
submerged in a cascade of spilled
Manhattans & Martinis
I stood up the theme of Darkness Recurring
Darkness
left it on the Corner of D & Nile, baby
I stood up to the Clear White Darkness
when the Is, Wasn't, yes I Did
As a reward Darkness stalked me
knew my every move
Bleached to Dark my private moments of hue
leaving a miasmic blanket
of dolor & shame
I paced as if in a cell
searching above the rooftops
the trees the tors & aretes
for the needed molecules of Legba power
Damballa juice, Legba- Simon Peter of Yoruba
The One with the Keys to the Highway's
defunct oasis, Bodhisattva of joyous rebirth,
Jaggarnath of The Mighty World Wide Wretched
maybe there's a few drops left
an energy and impulse
extravagant in my Youth
The sere concrete whispered cruel ironies
mocking the importance
I'd put on my work
all that scribbling & paper

mocking the vastness & import
I'd put on myself & my over worked words
Like an anchor necklace pulling
my eyes down to no answers to why
no what-fors, no coming froms
No coming, no bus
The bus isn't coming
Everyone in town is asleep
or gone home for the holidays
8.
9.
10.
The bus isn't coming
The final flight has flown in stealth
Where will I sleep it is quite cold
The gut-tired groan melts into a moan
Lacklove
I was as brave as a flat
gashed by a sharp
I had no lug matching spare in...
Not nowhere next to nowhere
No spare & the donut is flat somewhere in
The Great Salt Desert in
the middle, in the compassion-forsaken
literal middle, of the New Jersey Turnpike
tripping, peaking
O the fugacious fumes and spumes!
O the familiar dismal buzz & carbon bleak...
Stuck on the Gee Dub for hours...decades...
generations

It was the leaves of a calendar flying off
into the Never More
Always Less
The worshippers & practitioners of the
Outward Ceremony
never were there
never on the side of love justice compassion
when the silver bounced
on the table
Believers stabbed their eyeballs

declaring their unworthiness
They slurped vomit and killed for love
in one motion
But what of? O the great & pure lovers?
The cage rattling renegade misunderstood?
The workers who gave their lives
to honest work for less than
honest pay
The born impoverished who never had a chance
The mothers that wept joyless tears
for the wounded children of others?
The sons who never came home from the War

Let me confide in you
The Jesus, the Buddha
may have been great
But their words were always too late
The Sword struck while the Ordained Scribe
was trying to get a deal on ink
A century later his hard on & hard drive crashed
as the battery exploded
Vladimir's bullet was a white burn in the chest
another was mid-air
As the Spirit cardiologist
rosined her bow
The Sword traveled thousands of miles
while the magicians & logicians
self-satisfied bottom liners
were mixing their paints & measures
the new masters
Bridges of two-legged carrion
disintegrated into a confetti of flesh
Eyes shattered like shot windshields
Intestines as mulch randomly strewn
Super luminous strobic pulsing revealed
the source of the stench & it was ugleeeee
As the bridge builders assembled their
compassionate & humorous tools
& capital & codes
Suddenly they had to go home
for a forgotten essential, the password

and since then have been contemplating
whether an error is acceptable if it is human
which means what? humans are exonerated
before they err because that is what they do?
To err is human
But it was also written the saddest words are these
IT MIGHT HAVE BEEN
The overwhelmed bought something
from a store or what replaced Sears
& Monkey Ward
on line
just to remind themselves
they were alive

For some confusion was reassuring
an exoneration of do nothing & know less
"Viva Stalin!" they shouted as they
were mowed down in the Gulag
"Oh, only if Uncle Joe knew!"
They thought their Incarcerators, the firing squads
were counter revolutionaries!
The poor bastards believed in The Revolution!
They thought Stalin's goons were imposters
undermining The Revolution!

Nearly a Century later across the Oceans
the surmise sickens me
"It's all good," they smiled as they
were ripped out of their American Homes
"What me worry?"
They voted a Hitler admiring
Uncle Scrooge McDuck on Addies
invoking rage & bigotry as the muse, even called him
the Second Coming sent by God the Father
the latest very genius 2019 model
Nazi Jesus

The ones cursed with clarity shouldered
the dismal awakening
Like a cross far heavier
than boredom
When & then are now
but there's no How, no how
The Truth is a Killer
a hoax & a liar
The Truth is if it isn't territory
money or sex they'll fight
over words

They'll storm out to the parking lot
into the glove box in the Heart of Texas
and come back with "my big brother"
wielding him
barking over that's my pencil
that's my cup my shovel
a wutchoo looking at?
Screeching DIE!
Die you every vile venom word for you the Other
they spit kick slash and plug
They'll bring long knives onto the trains
machetes to The Corner
to the Hoe Down into the
bar, the convenience store, the school yard
movie theater, church
Assault rifles and Mr. Glock will rock out
coat pocket case anyone
disrespects them at the dance or shopping mall
case terminal frustration overwhelms them
and because of race religion & sexual hatred
They'll unleash automatic weapons
just to hear the staccato spondees
It's all they got left
The super human rumbling power joy ride
reveling in spectacular flash flooding
illumination firing fiery flying fragments
at what the Dead had built
that stood for centuries
They use flesh and blood to make video games real

Sign up now, wear super head phones
watch the cartoons explode
Get a uniform a badge get weaponized
You don't need a hood or mask
You don't need to take any backtalk
to make your nabe as safe & civil
as Ward & June
Wally & the Beav

The sex of Spring is brought hooded & shackled
before the tribunal sentenced
to burn and drown
drowned in fire burned in H2O
Yes perhaps lucky you be, a fortunate one
spared for use as sport or profit a border guard
an officer of correctional facility
or just instrumentum vocales
a tool with a voice

Geld has its guilt and is clever
in its disguise, some of its disciples
have mastered override of guilt
and use what is left
as an avenging weapon
Yes the twig that rules the meadow
is egoless and ultimately helpless
Soon the particulates of planet rot
shall morph into fertility killing offal
spewed from buried alive
misused earth crap poison bile
of sordid consequence, low filthy rotten...
dirty mother...big effing pus bag
I ran out of words, even those that curse

When Yo! Lo and Behold
Whence came out of Nameless Nowhere
an enormous FLASH! A tremendous preposterous
ffffFLASH! Glowing Growing and I saw
that I was wrong! So wrong, I erred
colossally enormously O forsaken
self... I was wrong!

I had been blind, now I see, suddenly seeing
it's Hilary! She'll get Wall Street in line
get big money out of elections
she'll keep us safe, help women achieve
and keep making good deals arming our
Wahab Saudi Arabian allies & deal with
Walmart Honduras Venezuela Libya Syria
Amazon and thee Amazon!
She's the one knows how to get it done
just like in the song, I was blind but now I see
Like digging Obama hipping us to how good things really are
he's set us up for years to come
Yes, Hallelujah, now I see, It is a placenta, a placenta in the sky!
A god damned mother fucking placenta
I see it clear as day
not the monthly blood and definitely not
the eructation of the Death industry,
not cancerous gestating filth
not the dross of battlefield hospitals
It's a Placenta, A Placenta!
A mystical immaculating Placenta emerging
from the home soil
infusing the air
manumissing grand old notions
nourishing our every fervor & desire
That's why I got this break--this vision
Sever and tie the cord & back to work

One foot, then another
Back to Work! Turn to! Hit it! Positivity!
Posterity
My visions of the Horror
were a ruse the produce
of Maya
I was letting my own despondency and
depressions suck the verdure
out of my crops
I saw the world in light of my own misery
I let my feelings override my mind brain judgment

experience
The world is not depressing me
I'm depressing the world and there I go again
It's my fault and I must atone
The only way I know
Back to Work!
Then is Now
When is How
Breaks Over...
Back to Work!

CODA:

Till I sweat Hudsons Columbias Missisips Sacramentos, Snakes
Amazons Niles Mekongs Yamunas Hallelujah
Back to work, Hallelujah
Till I shoulder a determined attitude like Simon of Cyrene
Back to work Hallelujah
Till I wei wu wei and wu wei wu all over you
Back to work Hallelujah
Till I'm not here and I'm not there, and the angel
in us lives, Hallelujah
I'll be working
When is now, I was blind but now I see
Limping is better than standing still
hit it

Breaks over. Hallelujah
Evil has gone cornball, down-home homey
Let your eyes swear they only see three when there are four
because that's where survival is
This is the Age of the Denied's Revenge
The worship of Revenge
The spilt drops demand more blood flow
Revel in the pain of others
Justice is a game you can't win
    you're beat before you begin

Be a winner look out for # 1
A little advice: Carry a copy of Fountainhead
in your pocket
Breaks over...!...
It was a placenta, damn, do you believe that?
a mama fucking placenta
Thee Prophesied Humanity Transforming
Placenta the cornucopia of mammalian
Flesh blood bones breath
O Yes Sing It Say It Live It
Hallelujah!

I Recall Reading It Can Be Done

I recall reading a pamphlet IT CAN BE DONE
A Carpe Diem type by a Dr. Frank Crane 1921

wrote one of the profoundest lines
that affected my life

"Today is the Savior crucified between two thieves
Yesterday & Tomorrow"

I haven't always lived up to the premise
of this metaphor

I've got to read the pamphlet again
but I can't find it

I'll try on line it was a pep talk in believing
the reward of effort is that one is consequential

It has muted out in me a defiant existentialism
The Wounded Warrior

The Poet who comes home to the Muse
without his heavy shield

The Muse wanted me to battle on
after the battle was decided

and the slaughtering began?
I must have ran, I left my sacred shield!

I'll go on blessed of the Muse or not
At this point I can't go back

IT CAN BE DONE
It must

WTF

I've seen a lot go under
ideas efforts that cost lives
artists masons carpenters outlaws
waitresses nurses factory hands farmers
school teachers moms fry cooks
their land, it's fair play & traditions
How can the health of our Home
our common Mother be regained
` and sustained
while lacklove violence
`` second nature cruelty, ravenous greed
networks unimpeded like a hyper super
virus invade the body of every nation
every clime, language & culture?
Everywhere money rules everywhere it circulates
which is everywhere
Why does everyone honor it, need it
jump to its demand?
What really backs it up
gives it value
Is open to conjecture debate & bewilderment
It would be really great to know
Can't be gold there's only enough
to cover a smidgen of the national debt
And besides you can't eat or drink it
A debt I was instructed we owe to ourselves
WTF

There's more money in cyberspace than
what is printed or coined
Is it guns, ideas, magic?
You'll be shot poisoned or starved
if you don't honor it?
WTF

They'll bomb each other
cut the throats, poison the water
Explode the babies & their mothers
land mines tanks white phosphorus the works

But the money is still honored, still traded
still valued, flows into & out of
warring nations

So what did the aging hippie say?
Can you envision it everybody?
Can you see it, everybody in the Woodstock
Nation helps each other be corporate free?
The aging hippie tells me so, tells me money
is not necessary is not the Future
Tells me that independent old time barter honesty
Will spread to the Hood & spread across META
Temporary Autonomous Zones everywhere
I ask, I know TAZ is great, but isn't it temporary?
Oh no the aging hippie avers more and more
every day down every way
It spreads across the vast brine, the rising seas
Into decomposing Africa, bleeding Mesopotamia
and exploding Afghanistan, Pakistan, Syria
burning hot thirsty Mother India
It saves the Amazon forest

I tell my friend that senior Flower Child
Go beat your head on a stone wall
Talk to the wall, write on the wall
It aint happening, doesn't have a snowflake's chance
in Hades
How could that happen?
The entire world history and consciousness
repeats WTF

Somebody must have & knows a plausible
Somebody could finish this piece
but it's beyond me
Give me a plausible, hope is still nothing
a scam to lull us into a Bermuda Triangle
of denial & suicidal apathy
I'd love to be a surprised one embarrassed
by my foolish pessimistic vision

my sordid outlook
Instruct me, how is it going to work out
into something lovely and plausible?
Damn sure I'll go along with it!
Is It plausible?
A plausible! Please...
WTF WTF WTF

In The Land Of Liberty

flowing through the cracks
The Zen and nourishment to see Buddha
on the passing trail smile in perfect harmony
moving on from her on the path
In
order to attain highest perfect enlightenment
Instead I blast the poet in me to smithereens
ripping it to dripping intestinal shreds
Just so this compost pile of verse will ferment
and shoot green towards the silver
energies caroming off my beloved
This is more than you know what for me
This will change my life even more
than you know it already has

Yeah, way down in, far out there, well
into It, honey, that's where I want to be
Where we're together again and money, money
is no object in the Land of Liberty

Bad Bald Eagle
– for Chris Funkhouser

Raise your fluted glass reflecting neon eyes
of the seventeen-year cicadas
Mistaken for unemployed bus boys & pearl divers
dancing high among the frozen roses
Blue in the silver night neath a slithering moon
the moon is mooning us
Let's laugh and guffaw praising
the Eternal Infinite Self-Born
Let the non-ending endure
true to itself without end
Let the Letts cavort in linguistic lettuce
see if I care
Let the rubles be inscrutable
Let the forints and kronas baht
yen pounds? euros dollars rupees
Be stapled together to make prayer flags
& kite tails
Glued together to make seed packages
so the Lilliputian mutants can hide
inside bananas and strawberries
As the frack water corn syrup marbleizes
a frown on the belly of Virtual Youth

We can stop melting icebergs with our Kindlings
Life has so much more reality these days
It's on TV every night
It's like butter or margarine
They are both real, amIrite?
Now we don't have to melt to inhale to feel
across a table of wine
We don't bother to communicate covertly

Because Ah Heck

They can know what we are doing in our kitchens
bathrooms bedrooms
Inside the physical heart toying with what flesh
inside the skull?

We're plugged in & so are the mysterious
ominous over powering They
Wired to exploit our desires and habits
The omnivorous appetite of cyberspace
will devour the language
New rebus like instructions will make
this language a foot note
Reality an unreal dose transforms the mind
into a city overwhelmed
by festering slag devotion
to gluttonizing the Finite

They must make absurd lethal non-sense moves
to maintain credibility in their unswerving
faith that their inequities & ridiculous
underpinnings of Control are justified
The earth is flat; industry doesn't affect the climate
As they make it appear it was some God
chose them gave them their cruel & brutal
talent that ordained them The Divinely Elect
Bosses of Economic World Murder

They use the Bald Eagle as a symbol
of their might is always right
Bad Bald Eagle doesn't care about other birds
Bad Bald Eagle doesn't care about other Bald
Eagles
unless he or she, it is usually he, craves
brick & mortar sex

He steals children, sometimes the body
sometimes mind often both
Bad Bald Eagle has a Bird Brain
yet rules the world
(cf. Allen Ginsberg)
With every move and word demonstrates
it does not have to make sense anymore
Meaning was put in a peculiar place where its denotation was   demoted
Bad Bald Eagle has seen to that

Bad Bald Eagle is a destroyer & despoiler
of language
Bad Bald Eagle believes, is invested in
dominance is virtue
He wants to be rewarded to be adored
for his exalting the lowest common
denominator
Bad Bald Eagle is very Bad
Bad Bad Bald Eagle Bad

Ace In The Hole

Yana & Me

You're my ace in the hole,
Vehicle, who I have named
Yana, I need you now

MUSIC BEGINS ROLLING

need you to understand, understand and how
To take these outpouring highways & overloaded
city streets as your lover
Let them hold you, know your smell and skin
as your wheels hump free & fast
miles miles and miles
of old to us wailing new mountains
Hardwood evergreens poplars fireweed glaciers
loggers miners hunters loners medicine men
Women frontier women
thousands of years of women
tireless treeless Tibetan Martian terrain
Don't fret you can bet there will be
a plenum of vast
petroleum swamps with restroom &
no-rest rooms
Hideous fluorescence like miasma
on the Nozone night
unearthly smoky salmon midnight
The golden nimbus of the buffalo graveyard
worked over
Great Plains breaks day with austere beauty
a foolish promise talking soil & air
robbing impossible prosperity
Double O hot lick stratocasters,
the sere dog lonesome
pining heart broke aint no joke fiddles flying
& crying the gore & lore of the jerkwater
podunk hardwood floor
Heavens exploding beer signs
Hollywood Nashville Vegas Dallas jukebox blue

jeaned social problems like atavisms
like the Cave
You got Vandals Lombards Visigoths Iberians Teutons Yoruba
Picts Angles Jutes Norse Kelts Etruscans Ovimbundu
Dravidians, Han, Magyars the Alpine race, Bogomils
Grimaldi, Cro Mags & Neanderthal
Is it the ethnic cleansing they call the distant past, that manifested
destiny, the dastardly victory they partake
they drive to drown the shame
in booze, lethal toys and mean ugly sex?

Hours of steep shale jack & white pine tent pole pine
rills wolds Montana sized flies: horse and deer
Boss sun shimmering off singing rails polished iron
hot enough to cook eggs on
Hooking supply & demand, Milwaukee with Seattle
and wherever she stops in between
But it can't keep up with us! Even so, gear it down Yana
we gotta go through Nevada's small towns where
everyone looks like a broken dream
a blackballed carny, a fabled failed prospector
Hit person on the lam, buzzard bait losers
who love the game more than themselves
Felonious women you can't imagine
being anyone's mom
Slot machines in the grocery Winnemucca
doomsday secrets over the arête deep
in the conclave of covert science
Steel birds breathing fire bullet through sound
broken sky lights
no Pharoah, no Iskander, no Sargon
could conceive illuminating
Reno & Tahoe every night
The smell of stockyards, slaughterhouses, coffee
diesel whiskey repeat melting plastic
The good scent of mown lawn is buried
in the sweat of escalating fear

The unmistakable odor of money selling itself
selling marriage divorce adultery pedophilia
Perpetual adolescent carnivals of onastic
images of suckcess
Sells children health religion education
sells water & electricity to Las Vegas
sells Alaska to Houston & Mitsubishi Japan
A piece of ten thousand steers went into your
burger
in El Paso in Jersey City makes no diff where
from the Amazon & the steroid mosh pit
Sells stolen property, private property is the altar
the church mammon as far as you can see
That's why we gotta get out of here, Old Yana,
tick tock the game is locked
there's nothing here for us
Now if you will notice coming up on our left
Vatos Locos on the ancient paint distorted stanchion
(that's a porch y'all)
Three dots and a cross, homemade homey tattooed hands
hands of yesterday
The deals gone done
the garden & wild mountains, the majestic plains
the no longer free undefiled water belongs
to a piece of paper
The sego lilies burst the desert
juiced roses cavort in the glazed eyes
of reflex lust ignorant till proven guilty
Magic lizards prosperous enuff to pay attention
to a dark pink Kirlian aura cloaking
the noirish riant ridge from where
we hear penitentes wail & wail
oooooooah, they can't get enough
Keep those RPMs in the drive it like you stole it
mode
Yana, roll roll it roll it up, stretch it, escape
vamoose yonondio AMF --
Think about the pain & confusion it takes
all the shit excitement & poison one has to eat

so the family survive
then notice:
the big horned ram more impressive
than a postage stamp looking stupid
in the middle of the road

SHORT INSTRUMENTAL:
TAKE A FEW SWIGS OF ICHOR

In another life our millionaire boss spent more money
than we make in a month to kill that Bighorn
There goes antelope 40 MPH under the fences of Destiny
so damn Manifest
Mama moose begins to panic as city dwellers
good naturedly corner her
The yellow eye coyote knows an automobile
is not a mammal
& guess just guess where we are?
roll roll it & rock rock it some more
down & up & smoke smoke it
And you know why we SHOOD smoke it?
because it is big, it is hot it's BIG
& it's so hot it's foreign
It's armadillo jack rabbit rogue horse
cases of Lone Star & Shiner
peons bros old boys
and good old gals in pickups
Rolling rolling rocking
bugs splattering asphalt steaming
undulating sweating road buckling exhaling
miraging every 30 minutes or so
just one word, "Texas"
maybe one more, "damn"
Desperate oak & shrub & scratch brush
plenty scorpions coral venom sidewinding
fearless buffed water bugs and buckets
of feral flowers bloom like cups & easter bonnets
human ears & distant stars
Cotton plants oil rig cotton plant sugar cane

oil rig sweat & more sweat & big buck cars
& suits & glass & cement & money
perspiring in bank vaults & accounts
in cyberspace
& fish are sweating in billion dollar
miscalculationary negligence sweating
long horns boots hats
Gotta have guitars gotta have live music
some kind of music
It was 95 when it rained this afternoon
six inches a cab driver said,
"That's good luck, all around."
Three alarm dancing hollering for more
what it's all about
beer & more beer & nachos
Love of the common people
All right everybody within the sound of my voice
we are blessed with rare experience
It is time to purchase and consume
the transcendent beer, the one that will get you
over & through
takes you to the other side
the Beer of Destiny
Step up to the bar, raise your hand at your table
this next beer is transubstantiated
the body & blood of the Divine Average
the Love of the Common People
It's a lot like America, no & yes
Tejas under the big bright stars

MUSIC: RAUCOUS HOT LICKS BOOGIE

But something is wrong mighty wrong
the disillusionment is mightier than the word
mightier than the beer & the weed
Won't let go won't hit bottom turns ugly
the hospitals police courts programs
nothing can keep up
Life as we know it and knew it
aint never coming back
aint only lost the essence of our metaphors

we lost our what fors, even worse
we've lost our laugh
that opens a Sacred Place
our solar plexus bursts forth
a laugh that does no harm that restores Ozone
that laugh is lost, gone, not happening

MINOR KEY LAMENT

Thru the evergreens the pines, the spruce, the firs
bathed in sparkling pogonip
Eat eyes the fruit of the Sumac
last resort of flying blood & feathers & bones
unearthly royal mauve velvet
Forbidden Planet fruit exciting our extremities
with thoughtless knowing
Iroquois mother wept fog reclaiming the land
soughing
thru the ess shaped spruce
of the legendary ice storm of 89
Cloudy marbles dropping thru fathomless
agate ocean of way-out ultramarine visible
Zaum beyond sense & intellect
phenombulating latescent banks
of skycumlation higher than we Yana
High

We'll fly south thru Binghamton at night
a great jazz station, it's Stuff Smith!
It's Slim & Slam & Bam: The real McVout
the essential Orooni
for a score of minutes
then static and gone
Lo Bo hey Joe Yonnondio Woe Ho
let's go Ah Hum let's go Yonnondio Joe
Soon we'll be filling our nostrils
with those fiery neoprene spumes
of Turnpike Jersey
The guts of the USA
The intangible so called Soul
of the USA

The ulcerated juggernaut & colon
of the USA
The old low down old-time low down
Immigrant dreams & promise
of the USA ah a backyard
The land of LOVE CANAL
& home bars under vanishing stars
& holy mother the car
of clean & dirty fun
the jukebox laughing
at the barking of a gun & spinning
red lights
Of ubiquitous gambling & porch rambling
and 5AM jammed rooms of drunken
would be & wannabe artists, music makers,
townies & clownies
unfit water & dandelion farms
Jets Giants Nets Devils army bases
weird Algrenesque factory lives
` envelope factories
glory days, buildings buildings
iron cement & glass
sated with managerial squelch production vassals
gaseous eyed waitresses with tears
tattooed on their crumpled faces
pick & shovel backs bent over
at the will
Big rig unloading deltoids traps & triceps
burger chains with the hapless penury
on both sides of the counter
the nervous sidewalks of No work Newark
This is home brutal lacklove newspapers blowing
in the wind, plastic stuck to cyclone fences
Coffee slugged! think of the kids
Into the world!
The shore, Long Branch--the beach
kids point out thousands of white shells
actually plastic tampon applicators, kids
into the world!

Driving driving driven
rolling rolling roll on
Yana into manyana rolling
Maryland West Virginia, Virginia
Smell the difference, swallow it feel it
feel it permeate your fibers of steel
up the Smoky Mountains
We hear the Dravidian Celtic moon fiddles
the ditties & laments of Catal Huyuk
The gasp of a bottle being opened
the echo of it being emptied
in your open wing
The song of the bitter young woman
now older, sadder & wiser
at great cost
The red dirt & tobacco
the big boys in cigar cars
The little old boys on side hill holdouts
mama's looking out the 4 square window
The wash the dinner the fights the kids
the drinking the food stamps the shit jobs
the broken water pump the rotted muffler
The tear in the roof, the siding paper
the small-town death of ideas
the cruelty of us in paradise
Yana, I want Cajun swamps with our old
socket sot hot samadhi eyes pirogue-ing
on the turtle running bayou
The red peppered gumbo & catfish fry
cry the low harp
wha wah wahwah wha hah wha-wa
Midst ogresome samsara bound refineries
brushing under living icon of the lonely:
sentimental hermetic willow
Weep for us we're going yonder
into the plains
We are driving diving into erosion
into rumbling ghost herds
into sky on fire
into the agony of the original people
The sawdust petroleum fattened corn fed

land burnt rangeless bovine feed lots
stenching the blanched horizon
going dark barreling away
Again thru jerkwater podunk poison Kool-Aid
freedom fried Red Dawn burger burgs
Corn sweetened vortices of native death
chicken crink crank cartwheels crystal
can't afford coke
Jukebox ancient video game meth death
no sanctuary churches of worshipped guilt
death & revenge death of a nation

JAZZ WILD JAZZ HOT JAZZ

Larry Clark's Tulsa
Danny Lyon's Huntsville
Sharon Doubiago's Hard Country
& big bag faced bears in plaid shirts
peripheral vision on the heavy metal
goldilocks goddess as the heaven's explode
over nature's best in a schooner
and no one sees it's a cheap trick done
with mirrors & the harnessing of a river
& Utah's french harp does sound
"like a lone bawling calf"
& Mary Jane's fiddle's been to school
& back & those bow hairs spangle
setting athrill the opaquing honky tonk
with its lamprey eyes & the restless rest
Where we seize the caesura
and deliver an old Walloon proverb
what goes in there must come out
We shake hands with Satan
in the mirror gone damp head
on the paint scaling walls
A crudely drawn double crescent
with curly hair around it
A subconscious expression of allegiance
to a gynocratic civilization
of prior bliss?
Over the toilet paper is scrawled

"Nuke the Iranian whales!"

Outside a porcine balding ox puts
a 16-inch sausage between his legs
And all his buddies snigger and guffaw
the chuckles fade out
there's an unfamiliar silence
the silence of the fan
the rock and roll Muzak
on stimulants as the 19-year-old daughter
of low rent housing hums and dances
feet not moving picturing Hollywood
like a show on TV like Dynasty
like Nashville Vegas Houston Honolulu
the Big Apple, maybe just Florida
in the New England winter
Or a cool guy with manners & money
or a ride with the soft soap seller
or the moon tanned violence camping
domineering ruthless heart breaker
who is so cute when he's cavalier
with screaming young bodies
who want him at all costs
He's kicking women off his steel studded leather
legs
We'll leave her dancing
we'll split the cenotaph bar & grill
we'll vamoose this side of nowhere

EAST MEETS WEST – PIANO PLENTY OF PIANO
IF POSSIBLE

We'll fire up & out, wake up in a rain of Xanadu
We'll find glass-eyed ponds
hours from asphalt
Where the smartest trout are wolves
The hatchery trout fat house dogs
in the mainstream
where prolific ferns put carnal ions
into the wired air
over & down shale faces & fences

living walls & escarpments
jumping the rocky rills
quickly unfolding wolds down to
where the boss sun shimmers
a warped film rising from the polished
iron rails where sweat sizzles
The last electric major railroad in the US
called the Milwaukee Road rattling by
Letting us gandy dancers lean on
our short shovel "guinea banjos"

SLAVIC-TARTAR JAZZ

We're running out of fuel
running out of money
but I have an idea
So here's the idea, Yana
to skulldig network manufacture a grant
yes an articulate proofread proposal
To visit all poisonous dump sites of America
legal & illegal
Don't worry we'll wear suits space age stuff
we'll hire immigrant refugees to get close
we got zoom cameras
To what purpose? Art!
let's brush sculpt film perform pen
a new real ashcan school
with a real populist punch!
Let's paint the sky the wrong colors
hues never seen before in the vastness
that literally inspires us
Let's really paint the sky
let's stain it
let's have it the way
we want it
like fast food
Let's exhibit the aesthetics of extinction
document it, document the process
give'em data with their tears
just as long as the checks don't bounce?
Expose beauty & art of visual guilt

stimulation of grotesque rampant cancers
We'll declare Beauty in the annihilation of Substance
and replace it with gold toilets
and pretty 3D copy machine Birds
and starlets & super-buffed youngsters
We'll display musical & thespian splendor
in the last gasps of expiring orbs
to clear cut bleed to the bone
perpetual usury world-wide wretched
We'll make it art by Jimmy

INSTRUMENTAL OF CHOICE

You question the paucity of my vision Yana?
You've been a Good Old Vehicle all these years
We're gonna gear it on down
let those old pistons and rings
hum the sentimental yesterdays
let their minds off

Let's get a sweet glide going
You're not a Mahayana
you're a plain old Yana
hardly pick you out from the others
I prophesy Maitraya will arrive in an ordinary Yana

So Blow Yana Blow Have your saxophone moment
You want to show me the grain still undulates
like an amber ocean
The dry autumn corn the land
where our children were born
Redwoods stand like living gods
older than Jupiter, Jesus & Mohammed
The ferns make the air electric
some beauty words can't place
Pikes Peak & Death Valley
7th & B and Harwood Alley
The Brooklyn Bridge
The Seattle Space Needle
The Cascades in June
The Valley of the Moon

Towers dwarfing pyramids & ziggurats
Babel a tinker toy compared
Highways to every and no where
arteries and capillaries in the sky
Choking waste and more waste
guzzling burning & spilling
disrupting what we know
is risky and dangerous without precedent
for the pleasures lucre will afford
now who cares about later now
An economy based on weaponry
where Mammonistas ride like a sacred proverb
Hundreds thousands millions billions from hand to mouth
paycheck to paycheck have refugees to remind them
there are fortunate to be slaves
Wage slaves no wage slaves, slaves to materialism slaves to
digesting lies, slaves to pipedream religion
slaves to digesting fear, slaves to revenge
Slave to the rent

Vehicle you & I know
We know why abundance is feared
We know why abundance is feared more than the Plague
more than Nuclear Death
Who'll do the dirty work?
Who'll do the unhealthy and perilous work?
The repetitive the boring the low paying
"if abundance be?"
It has to change

INSTRUMENTAL FAST BLUES

We know why Nature is Hated and Persecuted
Some say money is an exemption from hell
an exemption from SCARCITY
That's the American Dream, getting over
spending other's labor & misfortune

The Mighty Powers are afraid they 'll have to do
some of their own difficult dirty
tedious work if scarcity is not the motivator
An exemption from hell is an exemption
from SCARCITY
sure, it was different 500 years ago
who wants 500 years ago?
who really wants it?
who wants to hear it breath it
relive it? All that killing & grieving grief
Forget it Yana keep moving
over the bleached leeched topsoil
over the fetid channels
under Giardians skies & flying arsenals
around insect conquered cities
Millions upon millions unhappy with their sex
unhappy with sex their own & others
Millions of agendas to snuff us
to do in all we once loved
Keep rolling wind her up
the highway will be our sex
Wherever we stop seems like dream's memorial
We cry the labor's been abused enough
To the misfortunate misused marginalized
it's colder than a cold lover
Ground up plowed paved driven over spent
imagination ignored and its lack glorified
The heart's in a scrap pile, a childish notion
of the naive past
Truth a whimsical tyrant, an admitted falsifier
and the stench clouds are behemothic
and unavoidable permeating dyspeptic eructation
from a festering lethalizing breath
So go Yana go for the Maha, Yana drive into the sun
go to North & South Dakota stand with the Sioux
Go to the Valley of the Moon and see if J London's
alchuringa are readying for their entry
into the good old 21st Century
Go to Angola state prison and unshackle Leadbelly
zoom to Robert Johnson's crossroads
make Karen Silkwood survive live to

& in a redemptive age
Change the deal follow the underground railroad
To Canada up the Alcan to Alaska, Seward's folly
the Matanuska Valley experience
the legendary Thunder Fuck
Watch the salmon battle the falls at the mouth
of Ketchikan Creek
Watch the lady feeding 50 bald eagles
at the tip of Homer spit
We'll drive to Whitehorse and go outside
and wind up at Little Big Horn
and listen to the famished apparitions
We'll go to Rabbit Ears Pass and make love high
we'll go till our wheels fall off
we'll go to Walla Walla
what better place to wet our whistle
We'll go to Hoboken Ward Denver the Bay
Felton Vallejo Eugene Lowell Austin
Spruce Street Woodstock the Village
Back to San Jose Besprizoni Las Vegas!
A rolling contradiction, a laughing jukebox, under
vanishing stars, into sky on fire, waking
               in a rain of Xanadu
Yana into Manyana into Mahayana
the big brown cloud we will endure
we've no other choice
for the sake of cherished words
For the love of the Common People
for love for Love
Me & Yana with a brazen shout on our lips
MORE ROAD--LIFE-BRAVERY
THE ROAD THE ROAD
me and Yana holding hugging riding
THE ROAD

IF POSSIBLE SAME ROLLING MUSIC AS THE BEGINNING

Andy Clausen

Andy Clausen was born Andre Laloux in a Belgian bomb shelter in 1943. He was raised in Oakland, California. USA. He graduated from Bishop O'Dowd High School in 1961 and attended six colleges. An ex-marine, he is the author of 14 books of poetry, including 40th Century Man: Selected Verse 1996-1966 (Autonomedia, 1997), Without Doubt (Zeitgeist Press, 1991, introduction by Allen Ginsberg) and was coeditor of Poems for the Nation (Seven Stories Press, 2000), a collection of contemporary political poems compiled by the late poet Allen Ginsberg.

In 1968, he signaled the intensity of his enegetic spoken word recital for which he would become known and would affect the generation of latter-day beats as well as many writers of Generation X when he performed naked save for an American flag tie at the Conference Of Small Magazine Editors and Publishers in Berkeley. The following month, when Allen Ginsberg caught a glimpse of Clausen at the Rolling Renaissance readings in San Francisco, he thought he was seeing the young Neal Cassady. Allen Ginsberg not only called him the "Future of American Poetry" but in the introduction to Without Doubt, said he would take a chance on a "President Clausen."

Clausen has taught at Naropa University and given readings and lectures at many universities, prisons, poetry conferences, and cafes at home and around the world. He has worked for poetry in the schools agencies in California, New Jersey, Colorado and New York. His memoirs of his friendship and adventures with Allen Ginsberg, Gregory Corso and many others of the Beat Generation was published as "BEAT The Latter Days of the Beat Generation A First-Hand Account" in 2018.

In 2020 Andy was named State of New York Beat Poet Laureate by the National Beat Poetry Foundation, Inc.

In 2021, Andy Clausen was honored again by the National Beat Poetry Foundation with the title, Lifetime New Generation Beat Poet Laureate.

"Inherited Neal Cassady's American Energy Transmission" - Allen Ginsberg, New Directions 37"... the frank friendly extravagance of his metaphor & word-connection gives Andy Clausen's work a reading interest rare in poetry of any generation."
- Allen Ginsberg, Deliberate Prose

Andy Clausen - NY, USA
New Generation Beat Poet Laureate
(2021-Lifetime)
State of New York Beat Poet Laureate (2020-2022)

Photo credit © Marian Tortorella 2024

www.ingramcontent.com/pod-product-compliance
Lightning Source LLC
Chambersburg PA
CBHW071152090426
42736CB00012B/2307